NAKED

By

Romella Vaughn

To: Yvonne

May God continue
blessing you!! I can't
wait to see what God is going
to do with!!

Love,
R

Acknowledgements

This book would not have happened without God. He showed me that I could do anything that's put before me. So I have to acknowledge Him first. He was with me the entire time on this journey. He ordered my steps, protected and provided for me, gave me a chance when no one else would, never betrayed me, listened when I needed someone to talk to, looked past all of my flaws, and most of all, loved me unconditionally.

I thank God for placing intelligence and positivity into my life. Thanks for showing me favor and teaching me new things. I know that You're not done with me and You're going to take me down other avenues. I'm truly thankful for everything that You have done for me throughout my entire life.

This book would not have been possible without the support and encouragement of my husband, Jude S. Vaughn, Sr. You always love me and support every decision that I've made. In spite of the physical pain that you have endured and long hours at work, you always made sure that home was taken care of. Thank you also for being patient with me while in the process of writing this book, I love you and I always will!!

My father, Randy Holmes Sr., who raised four kids on his own and loved us unconditionally.

Words cannot express my gratitude to author April Dishon Barker for her professional advice. I thank you for being a mentor, book coach and for your assistance in polishing this book. Thank you for teaching me how to humble myself at all times. (I watched you when you least expected).

I want to thank Percy Ray Bryant III, A.M.P. Marketing and Pray by Percy Ray Clothing for helping me design this book. I thank you for being patient with me.

I would like to give a special thanks to my children, Kentrell Holmes and Jude S. Vaughn, Jr. for understanding my long nights at the computer. I love you and pray that God will be with the both of you.

This book is dedicated to:

My Heavenly Father.
My husband, Jude Shawn Vaughn Sr.
My father, Randy Holmes Sr.
My late mother Patsy Kador, whom I miss dearly
My late brother Germaine Holmes, whom I miss dearly.

Table of Contents

Chapter One – Stuffed

At the beginning of the summer in 2014 I did something that I'd never done before in my life. I went to God in prayer and asked Him a simple question. "What is my purpose in life?"

He didn't answer right away. It was on one smoldering hot, summer day, while working as a letter carrier that He spoke to me and placed it in my heart to write a book based on my life experiences.

I thought about what I'd been through in my life and there were many things that came to mind. Most of which had caused me to feel heartbroken, broken in spirit, hurt, disappointed, unworthy and sometimes wishing that I were dead. I thought to myself, *I have a story to tell.*

As the summer went by, God woke me up on several occasions in the early morning hours. One particular time He showed me a vision of me speaking to millions of people, both men and women, about my life experiences. I wept and thanked God for what He was showing me.

One day while preparing my mail for delivery, God flashed before me that same vision again. My eyes watered and I was excited because I knew that God was going to use me in an awesome way. I knew from that point that I had to bring change into my life so I prayed to God that He would send a God-fearing Christian and mentor into my life.

At the end of the summer I began to get discouraged because I hadn't received an answer to my question from God. Then, on October 2, 2014 at 1:16 A.M. something astonishing happened; God gave me an analogy. I saw a vision of a stuffed teddy bear. He told me to remove all of the cotton from the stuffed animal. Then He told me to think back to when I was a little girl up until now, 41 years of life, and to re-stuff it for every hurt, disappointment, regret, setback, frustrations, etc., that had affected me and that I'd never discussed with anyone.

I thought about the hurt I felt when my mother gave my siblings and me to my father and how it made me feel abandoned, rejected and motherless. I stuffed it. Watching my dad being used by demonic forces, and it causing him to do things that a normal person wouldn't, left me feeling alone, afraid, helpless and desperate for someone to turn to. So I stuffed that. Being a mother-figure to my siblings at the young age of ten, my childhood was taken away. I stuffed that, too.

Being betrayed and hurt by friends left me feeling unable to trust anyone. Being lied on by co-workers left me wanting revenge. Carrying others' burden and solving their problems left me feeling exhausted. I stuffed all of these emotions as well.

Before I realized it, I had ran out of cotton and needed more to stuff the teddy bear for all of the pain that I had endured. After completing this task, the brown bear, which represented me, was bursting at the seams. God revealed to me that I had lived my entire life tucking and stuffing my hurt and pain, never releasing it.

My heart was heavy and I wept. I couldn't understand why all of these things had happened to me. He revealed to me that I went through it all for a reason and that He was always there to protect me.

He said, "Romella, it's not about you, it's about helping others. Your story will heal people all over the world that are hurting and have never talked about their pain or did anything about their hurt." The wells of my eyes watered and I wept tears of joy. I had a better understanding of why my life went the way that it had. Then it was time for the healing to begin.

On October 7, 2014 I received a call from a close friend who was having problems with her husband. As I listened to her, I realized that she was feeling hopeless. She couldn't understand why her husband was neglecting her. God used me to minister to her. I explained to her that her husband was being used by the enemy to attack her—it wasn't him. I told her that we needed to pray and rebuke the spirit that was trying to destroy her marriage.

After she hung up the phone, she sent me a text saying that she appreciated me and that I was a blessing. Reading those words made me feel good. It confirmed for me that God wanted to use me to encourage others.

Later that morning I asked God how He wanted me to write a book to encourage others when I still had issues that I needed to deal with. After all, I was still struggling with all of the things that my husband had done to me.

He took me back to a conversation I'd had earlier with my girlfriend and used the very same words for me that I had said to her, "The enemy was using your husband to attack your marriage." He told me that I needed to express my feelings to my husband and explain to him how his actions affected me for so many years.

God dropped in my spirit that I needed to let the past go because it couldn't be changed. And that He was going to heal me through the process of writing my own book. I felt a sigh of relief and burdens were lifted off of my shoulders.

In the process of me writing "Naked," I received a call from a close friend that had some concerns about his 50-year-old girlfriend. He said that she was questioning him about his ex-girlfriend and that she was insecure. He had forgotten that he'd told me when he met her, she'd explained to him that she was insecure because of past relationships. She had never felt loved by her family, didn't feel pretty and was looking for acceptance. I thought to myself, *he called the right person.*

I told him even though she had learned how to fix herself up on the outside, it didn't mean that she had dealt with her issues on the inside. It had taken me forty-one years to realize that I was still holding on to hurt. Just imagine what she's most likely going through at 50 years old. He told me he never looked at it that way but that I was absolutely right. I asked that he utilize his patience and be more understanding to how she feels. I laughed because now, here I was giving relationship advice.

Living your life holding on to the hurts of the things done to you that you never discussed with anyone is not healthy. It is more dangerous than you think. These things that you have tucked and stuffed do not only affect you, they affect those around you. The pain from unresolved issues can cause you to make bad choices, saying and doing things that bring even more destruction. You may also become spiteful, be mean and hateful, live a long, bitter life and take it to the grave or worst of all, commit suicide.

Different types of activities people use to cope with while being stuffed with hidden hurts are food, sex, drug, alcohol and abuse to cover up how they really feel. Could this be you? If so, are you ready to unstuff? Meaning, are you ready to heal by emptying yourself of those hurts and laying naked before God, letting Him clothe you in love and righteousness?

If you are going through trials, I suggest that you pray about talking to a counselor. Professionals are trained to walk you through the healing process. Another option is talking to a relative or close friend that you trust. First, use the analogy that God gave me. You'll be surprised to discover all of the things that caused you to tuck and stuff over the years. Whether you used stuffing as a method of self-protection or simply a coping mechanism, you can stop today. God is right there with you in this process.

Are you ready for Him to give you a garment of praise in exchange for the spirit of grief? If so, pray this prayer with me.

Heavenly Father,

I am stuffed and I am so full that I am ready to explode. I am accepting the fact that it is time for me to change; to be healed by Your powerful love. Here I am. Please heal me. In the name of Jesus, Amen.

Here are some scriptures that helped me as I walked through the process myself.

Scriptures
Philippians 4:6-7

"Be careful for nothing; but in every thing by prayer and supplication with thanksgiving let your requests be made known unto God. And the peace of God, which passeth all understanding, shall keep your hearts and minds through Christ Jesus." (KJV)

Matthew 11:28-30

"Come unto me, all ye that labour and are heavy laden, and I will give you rest. Take my yoke upon you, and learn of me; for I am meek and lowly in heart: and ye shall find rest unto your souls. For my yoke *is* easy, and my burden is light." (KJV)

Chapter Two – Forgiving

When God told me to write this book, He didn't tell me how much it was going to hurt. I thought tucking and stuffing my past hurts would help me forget about them, but I realize how much they affected me in different ways. I was unsure where to start with my healing process. So, I started right where I advised you to start in the previous chapter. After I prayed about it and committed to begin the healing journey, I talked about it.

The most important person that I talked to was my husband. I had to be sure that he knew how I had been affected by the things he had done to me. When I sat down with him, my heart was pounding and racing because I didn't know how he was going to respond to what I had to say.

One of the major issues that we faced as a couple was when my husband was unfaithful so the first thing I did was explain to him how his infidelity shattered me. I told him that it left me feeling insecure, ugly, not good enough and rejected. I shared how it changed the way I viewed him and how I no longer trusted him.

I had brought a lot of baggage from past relationships into my marriage, which as a result, caused me to not be able to trust. I was hoping that he would protect my heart at all times, but he failed me. I explained how I felt open to commit adultery because of his betrayal. I felt like he "forced me out in the streets." In other words, he left me feeling unloved in my own home, causing me to look outside of our home for the love

I should have been receiving from him. I told him how even though the affair made me feel good at the time, I was really trying to fill that void left when he cheated on me. I just didn't care at the time. Now we had discussed all these things before, but something about the conversation was different this time. I apologized for not being faithful and asked him to find it in his heart to forgive me. God was moving in my heart to really forgive.

He told me he could tell that I no longer felt the same way that I did when we first met by the way that I responded to him, and that he'd done a lot of things to hurt me and was sorry.

Ultimately, I told him I was going to change and I would prove it to him in time. I declared that I was not the same Romella that I used to be. I know now that I'm beautiful and smart. I loved myself and was confident and I was not accepting anything less than a full commitment. I told him that through the dysfunction I stayed with him for various reasons, including for the kids. I was also afraid of being alone and did not want to be a single parent again.

I didn't want to just focus on the negative so I told him how much I appreciated him for never turning his back on his family and always making sure that we were taken care of. I also assured him that I was going to work on myself, as well as learn to trust him again since I'd decided to stay. I told him that besides all of his mistakes, he was a good man with a big heart.

One of the things that I realized about "stuffing" is how selfish it is when you're in a relationship. When you are hurt and broken, you cannot be fully present in relationships. Due to my selfishness, I never asked him how he felt about me committing adultery. So, since the conversation was started, I decided to ask him some questions.

I got around to asking him if he looked at me the same way. I also wanted to know how he felt about me committing adultery. His response was that he was wondering when I was going to ask him that question because he always thought that I didn't have any room to talk about being faithful once I decided to cheat. He summed it up by saying that he forgave me and was hoping that I'd done the same. What I've realized is that we may say we forgive, but deep down within, sometimes we really don't. I promised him that I would try my hardest to make our marriage better and work on me. I knew from that point, I had to move on. His forgiveness, solidified my decision to forgive.

I thought to myself, *why didn't I do this long time ago?* I do believe that everything happens for a reason and God will use my situation to heal and help others. God wants all of us to walk in humility and love, stop stuffing, get naked and forgive.

Forgiving someone can be difficult for many reasons. First of all, we like to talk ourselves out of its necessity. We justify our resistance with questions like, "How can I forgive a person that deeply wounded me?" or "Why should I forgive when it wasn't my fault?" We also don't want to be viewed of as weak and may wonder, "If I forgive, won't that make me look stupid?" Forgiveness is an integral part to moving forward and shouldn't be put off. Are you ready to forgive?

The fact of the matter is forgiveness is not for others, but for our own spiritual growth and healing. Love and forgiveness cannot be separated. Forgiveness is contagious. (Ephesians

4:32). If we choose to walk in love and fulfill the purpose of God in our lives, then forgiving others is not an option.

Heavenly Father,

I come before You to ask You to heal me from the things that have been holding me in bondage. I ask that You help me to forgive those that have hurt me. I pray Your blessings for those that have sinned against me. I pray that You bring positive and saved people into my life. God, direct me to the person that is trustworthy and use them to minister to my heart. Dull the sharp edges by reminding me that You are working everything out for my good, no matter how bad it may seem at the time. God, forgive me for not forgiving and for hurting the people that I've hurt. In the name of Jesus, Amen.

Scriptures
Matthew 6:14-15
"For if ye forgive men their trespasses, your heavenly Father will also forgive you.   But if ye forgive not men their trespasses, neither will your Father forgive your trespasses." (KJV)

Ephesians 4:31-32
"Let all bitterness, and wrath, and anger, and clamour, and evil speaking, be put away from you, with all malice: And be ye kind one to another, tenderhearted, forgiving one another, even as God for Christ's sake hath forgiven you." (KJV)

Isaiah 53:4-5

"Surely he hath borne our griefs, and carried our sorrows: yet we did esteem him stricken, smitten of God, and afflicted. But he was wounded for our transgressions, he was bruised for our iniquities: the chastisement of our peace was upon him; and with his stripes we are healed." (KJV)

Chapter Three – My Sacrifice

I can remember running up and down the concrete sidewalk of my Gretna, Louisiana neighborhood at the age of five. With my skinny caramel-colored legs and long, dusty-brown ponytails, I played with my neighborhood friends while my mom sat in the doorway drinking her Budweiser. We lived in a fairly small two-story apartment complex. My mom made sure that my siblings and I ate and kept us well put together the best that she could.

Things changed when my mother started to do drugs and consume more alcohol than normal. She dated a guy that lived across from us who was strange and mean. The two of them would fuss and fight, which caused me to be afraid of what might happen next.

One day, as my siblings and I slept, I heard a noise. When I opened my eyes, I saw my mom's boyfriend climbing through our bedroom window with a shotgun. He crossed over our twin beds and went into the living room where my mother was. The two begin to argue and fight. I thought to myself, *he's going to kill my mom*. Even though he had a shotgun, it didn't stop her from cussing him out and fighting back. Eventually, she was able to get him to leave and I was relieved. Just like other times, I admired that she never backed down from a fight with him, no matter how many black eyes she walked away with.

As my mom's drug and alcohol abuse worsened, she became violent. She had it out with almost everyone in the apartment complex. One night she was drinking heavily, I'm not sure if she had also been doing drugs or not, but she came in our bedroom while I was asleep and began beating on me. I cried out loudly, asking, "What did I do?" She called me all kinds of profane names and said that she couldn't stand me. She picked up my toy cash register and threw it at me, breaking it. I cried and cried. I didn't understand why she was doing that to me. When she was sober, she was the sweetest person. But when she was high, we never knew what was going to happen.

My mom had another close guy friend that lived upstairs from us and I would visit him daily. Mr. Smith was a diabetic and would take his insulin everyday around the same time, so I would make sure that I was there just to see him poke himself in the stomach with a needle. For some reason that was exciting to me.

One particular day he grabbed me by my hand and pulled me close to his private area and started feeling on me. As a child I didn't understand what was going on, but I knew something wasn't right. I can remember going down the stairs confused. After that day, Mr. Smith didn't have to worry about me visiting him anymore. I never told my mom what happened until my late teens.

At the age of six, I overheard my mom talking to my dad on the phone one morning. She told him she couldn't take care of 'these children' anymore and she was putting all four of us in a cab. Even though my mom had problems and wasn't perfect, I didn't want to leave her. Minutes later, I heard a cab blowing outside of the front door. My mom put my 6-month-old brother, my 2-year-old sister, my 4-year-old brother, and I in the cab. She gave the driver my father's address, which was actually my grandmother's home.

Upon arrival, I remembered my dad coming outside in his robe to pay the cab driver and to get us. I knew my father well but I had never lived with him without my mother. My siblings had no clue what was going on but I knew things would never be the same.

My grandmother had a small, simple house with one way in and one way out. My dad slept in the living room, which was the first room when entering the house. My dad explained to us right away that he didn't want us to leave that room, I guess to keep us from bothering my grandmother and running around the house. We weren't even allowed to use my grandmother's bathroom. He told us, "If y'all have to us the restroom, use it in this bucket." So, if we had to do the number two, we had to use it in the bucket and he'd go empty it into the toilet.

I didn't know my grandmother very well because we hadn't visited her often. As time went by I developed a pretty good relationship with her. She would keep me home from school just to go grocery shopping with her. When I was home alone with her, she would let me come into her bedroom and I would watch her as she sat on the side of the bed smoking her Pal Mal cigarettes without the filter. She made smoking cigarettes look fun.

One day when my cousin was visiting, we stole a couple of our grandmother's cigarettes. We went in the back yard under the house and lit the matches and fired up the cigarettes. When we took our first puff, we coughed and choked uncontrollably. We finally got the hang of it and it was on. We pretended like we were smoking Virginia Slim cigarettes, which made us feel sophisticated.

When we heard our grandmother call our names, we put the cigarettes out immediately and ran inside. We entered the house and walked over to her slowly because we knew we smelled like smoke. She made us open our mouths and blow. She said, "I know how many cigarettes I had." Smokers always seem to know how many cigarettes they have left in the pack. She threatened to tell my daddy and I was petrified because I knew he didn't play. When my father got home, she told him what we'd done and of course he whipped my butt. One thing about my dad, he was strict and heavy on the discipline.

About a year or so later, my dad found us an efficiency apartment. I hadn't seen or heard from my mother but I thought about her often and hoped she would come visit. We only had one big room that served as a living room, bedroom and kitchen and then one bathroom attached. My dad purchased some black paint and painted the word "Jesus" on the wall, which seemed strange to me. Every morning he would wake us up around 5:00 A.M. to pray. He was a very religious man that loved the Lord.

When it was time for me to go to school, my father and I together combed my hair. One would bush my hair to the back and hold it in place, and the other would tie the ball to secure it. And then off to school I went. When it was time to take a bath, he would put all four of us in the tub at the same time. He took his time and bathed us one by one. I always wanted to be the first one because I didn't want to sit in my siblings' dirt.

Not having a woman around made me sad at times. When my dad's lady friend would come over, that made my heart smile. It felt great having a woman in the house with us. She was sweet and treated us as if we were her own kids. When she came she would bring her kids and they stayed for days. I hated to see her go and would ask, "When are you coming back over?"

In spite of my loneliness at home, school was my comfort zone. It gave me a chance to be me, not the Romella without a mother, but just Romella. I was able to make friends very easily and that always felt good. It felt normal. Being able to play outside at recess with other girls my age was fun and let me act my age. One dark cloud in this otherwise sunny spot in my life was the sadness that enveloped me when I would watch other kids with their mothers.

As time passed, my dad received a Section 8 voucher for a three-bedroom house. We were all excited when we moved into a new and bigger place than what we were used to. This happiness was short lived, however, because my dad started doing things he had never done before. He started talking to himself and arguing with someone who wasn't there. He had become paranoid, always looking out of the window and accusing someone of trying to kill him.

At the age of eight or nine, my dad took me into the room by myself and asked me if the two lesbians that lived a couple of houses down were molesting me. They were a very nice and polite couple that never bothered anybody.

Emphatically, I told him, no. He insisted I tell him the truth. I tried to assure him that they never touched me but he wouldn't let it go and paced around the house looking at me strangely, asking me the same questions over and over again.

One day my dad took me to the hospital to see if I'd been touched. He wanted to make sure that I was telling the truth and I wanted him to take me so I could prove to him that nothing happened. I couldn't understand what was happening, but I knew that my dad wasn't the same person. When we arrived at Children's Hospital, my dad told the doctor that he thought that I had been molested and was no longer a virgin. The doctor took me in the exam room with his assistant. After the exam, he called my dad into the room and said, "Mr. Holmes, this child has never been touched." I felt a sigh of relief.

My dad looked at the doctor as if he were lying. On our way home on the bus, I looked up at my dad and said, "Daddy, I told you that I was telling the truth." He looked at me with this strange look on his face and then turned away. He didn't have much to say.

As days went by, he started waking me up in the early morning around 2:00 A.M., asking me the same types of questions. I was uncomfortable and tired of the questions. I thought to myself, *maybe if I tell him that they'd touched me, he'll leave me alone.*

One night he asked me over and over again until I became agitated. I said, "Yes! Yes, they touched me." He acted as if a bell had gone off in his head and asked what they'd done to me and if they'd stuck something inside me. I told him, no, but that they'd gotten on top of me and moved up and down. He was furious! He said, "We are going to the police station in the morning.

My heart dropped. I thought to myself, *Lord, what did I just do*? The next morning he took me to the police station and told the officer he wanted to file a report on the two women who'd touched his daughter. When the officer took me in a room by myself, he asked me to tell him exactly what happened.

I sat there and stared at the officer. Finally, I took a deep breath and swallowed. It felt like I'd swallowed a bag of marbles. I said, "Officer, I've never been touched. I don't know why my dad is acting the way that he is. I told him that no one touched me, but he doesn't believe me. I thought if I told him what he wanted to hear, he'd leave me alone."

The Officer called my dad into the room. He said, "Mr. Holmes, you don't have a case. Your daughter told me that she has never been touched. Here's my card, call me if you have any questions or concerns." My dad took the card and looked at the officer with a strange look on his face, but kept quiet.

The way the officer looked at my dad, I could tell that he knew my father wasn't in his right state of mind. My heart was beating uncontrollably and I wanted to vomit. I said to myself, *I know I'm going to get it.* He was quiet the whole ride home, which was shocking to me. I knew it was going to be a long night but fortunately after that day, he didn't mention anything else about it.

There were times when I looked at my siblings and wished that I were them. I couldn't understand why he was doing this to me: tormenting me with accusations of things that never happened and placing adult responsibilities on me as a small child. It seemed to me, my siblings didn't have a care in the world and enjoyed life.

I kept this tight knot in my stomach and was constantly wondering what was going to happen next. I wanted someone there just to hold me and tell me that everything was going to be okay. I wished that my life were normal like everyone else's. I felt like I was in a shell by myself.

One day my dad packed our clothes and said that we were leaving because somebody was out to kill him. We left our nice and comfortable home for what turned out to be no reason at all. We walked the streets until sunset and finally my dad stopped by this guy's house that he knew and asked if we could spend the night. The guy excitedly welcomed us in.

As the night went by, I could hear the guy asking my dad to have sex with him. My dad was furious and shouted, "I'm not a homosexual and I don't appreciate you asking me to sleep with you."

I was so afraid because I thought they were going to fight. I could hear the guy apologizing constantly. The next morning, after we left there, we went over to a family friend's house. My dad asked if it was okay for us to stay until he found a place for us to live. And that's what we did.

After we moved into our new home, another one of my dad's friends, Drew, asked if he could spend a night over because he didn't have a ride home. Once my dad told Drew he could stay, he instructed my sister and me to sleep on the sofa bed with him. My dad wanted to keep an eye on us. My brothers slept in their room and Drew slept in one of the rooms in the back.

The next morning my dad asked me why I had gotten up in the middle of the night and went to the back. I told him that I didn't and that I'd slept the whole night. Of course, he accused me of lying and I thought to myself, *here we go again.* Finally, my little sister said, "Daddy, I got up to go to the restroom." I was so relieved that she had spoken up.

I said, "Daddy, I told you that it wasn't me." I thought that he would leave it alone but he wasn't trying to hear it. He insinuated that I'd gone into the room with Drew, who was in his late twenties. He asked if Drew had touched me. After I tried to plead my case, my father went to the back of the house to confront Drew anyway. Drew denied everything but the two got into a huge argument. My dad asked him to leave and to never come back.

After years of not working, my dad finally found a painting job. We all thought that his boss, Mr. Tim was a nice guy. He had the upmost respect for my dad. He would pick him up daily and drop him off because my dad didn't have a car. One day my dad came home angry. He paced the floor and peeped out of the window all night. He said, "Tim hired someone to kill me." He mentioned that he and Mr. Tim had gotten into a huge argument. I don't think Mr. Tim knew of his instability. A few days later he returned to work like nothing ever happened. But the cycle kept repeating itself. Finally, Mr. Tim got tired of my dad accusing him of hiring someone to kill him, so he let him go.

As a young child, as young as nine to ten years old, I had many responsibilities. I had to make sure that the house was cleaned; I cooked, cared for my siblings and made sure my sister's hair was combed. If I didn't have those things done, I would get into some serious trouble. I always played the mother role, acting as if I was in my late teens or early twenties. I would hear friends and family say, "That's a strong little girl." But, they didn't know the pain I was in.

When my dad worked, he didn't allow us to go outside to play until he came home from work. We would sit in the window around the same time every day waiting for him to turn the corner. When we saw him we would jump up and down and say, "My daddy is coming! My daddy is coming!" We were so excited because we knew once he walked in he'd let us go outside and play.

My siblings would run up and down the street with their friends but I could never go to my friend's houses, they had to come to mine because I had to stay in front of the house so he could watch me at all times. As I played with my friends, I would turn around and see my dad peeping at me out of the window, making me feel uncomfortable. When the sun was shining, I was happy. But as the sunset, I would get this sick feeling in my stomach because I knew once I went inside, later that night, he was going to start tripping. I couldn't understand, for the life of me, why.

From time to time my mother would visit us. She came with snacks and gave us money. She would tell my dad that she wanted her kids back. I remember hearing my dad saying, "You're not getting my kids back." The two would argue and my mom would sucker punch my dad. He never hit her back and would just hold her down, telling her to leave. She threatened to put us in foster care and we were terrified.

I would say to myself, *here we go again.* I loved her, but having her around made me afraid because I knew she would drink and act up. As a teenager, it struck me that I knew in my heart she loved us, but it was hard for her to show it because of her addiction.

My mother met this guy by the name of Sam and quickly moved in with him. Sometimes we would visit them. Sam was an older guy who worked steadily and gave her money. Every time I saw them they were fighting and she would walk away with a black eye or two. When they came to pick us up for the weekend, I knew in my spirit that something bad was going to happen once she started drinking.

One particular weekend she came by to pick us up. My siblings were excited, but not me. When Mr. Sam stopped at the corner store to get some beer, I felt uneasy. Later that night I heard my mom screaming and yelling. We ran into the room and saw her lying between the bed and the nightstand while Mr. Sam beat her face continuously. When he finally stopped, both her eyes were swollen and she had a busted lip. When I saw my mom's face, it broke my heart. I had seen her with plenty of black eyes before but this was my first time actually watching her being beaten and it was a horrifying experience. I was angry with Mr. Sam and didn't like being around him because of what he had done to her. She cried and cried. The next day, as she sat on the bed with some witch hazel and a towel, she acted as if nothing ever happened. That confused me horribly. When I was with my mom, the only thing I thought about was being home with my dad. How ironic.

We spent years on food stamps and lived in Section 8 housing that was infested with rats and roaches. When we were kids, my siblings and I had a system that the first person that woke up would shout out, "I got the TV," and that person controlled the television the entire day. Sometimes, just to have control of it, I would say, "I woke up at five o'clock and called it, but everyone was sleeping." Therefore, I was in control for that day.

In my early teen years I knew that I didn't want to live my adult life the way I had as a child. Coming up we didn't have much. My dad did a lot of sacrificing to make sure that we had what we needed. Most of the clothes that we had were given to us by a relative or was donated. We all slept on one mattress on the floor and had one television. We had a table with no chairs and a few other odd pieces of furniture.

I had a friend when I was in the sixth grade and when I would go over to her house I saw well-coordinated, beautiful furniture that was neatly in place. Each room had a television and beautifully dressed beds, along with a dresser, chest, lamps and a nightstand. The walls were filled with beautiful pictures and a family portrait. And I didn't see one rat or roach crawling around. Her mother would be in the kitchen cooking their dinner and I wished that I had that life. Everyone appeared to be so happy. When it was time to go home, Lord knows that I didn't want to leave. I imagined that it was my home. I knew in my heart that I wanted more than what was handed to me. I didn't have an idea how, but I knew that it was going to happen.

As the years went by, my dad would disappear with no one knowing his whereabouts. My siblings and I stayed with my mother's sister once, and my dad's sister on two different occasions. The two of them were single parents and struggling to make ends meet. They did what they could to make sure that we were well taken care of in the midst of their own struggles. Even though I loved my father with all of my heart, I was happy to stay with my aunts because of their mental stability.

Living with my dad's sister was very different than livin
with my dad. I was able to have freedom after school wi
fewer responsibilities. No longer being under my father
watchful eye, at the age of 15 I lost my virginity tc
neighborhood boy. There was something about him 1
captivated me. He made me smile and even though we were
both young, being with him made me feel secure and wanted.
Having sex was uncomfortable, but I did it because I really
liked him and I thought that he would fall in love with me. I
was too young to really understand what I was doing at the
time.

Of course, it didn't last. I was lonely, broken and confused
when it was over. When the thrill was gone and we went our
separate ways, I felt unloved. In my search for love, I thought
that having sex was the way to find it. While trying to fill that
void, I became promiscuous, not realizing that I was adding
salt to my open wound.

My dad called and said he wanted his kids back but I didn't
want to leave. At the age of 18 I decided to stay with my aunt
while my siblings resided with my dad. I was pregnant and
didn't know how I was going to explain it to my dad. At the
time, I was working at McDonald's trying to save money
because I knew that I would need to care for my baby.

One day while working I received a call from my dad. He
told me that I had to come home because someone had broken
in and tried to feel on my sister. I said, "What about my job?
You live too far away, how will I get to work without
transportation?" He said I needed to come home because he
was working the night shift. My heart started pounding and I

began crying. However, this time I was not mad; I was furious. Once again, I moved home because I felt obligated. The cost to commute on the bus would cost more than I made and would have taken too long. I had to quit my job.

It was when I was 19, after I had given birth to my baby boy, that my dad came in my room to tell me that I had to now care for my siblings because he was leaving. His plan was to take me to the HUD office so he could pass the Section 8 voucher to me.

I said, "WHAT? What do you mean you're leaving? I have my own baby to care for." I didn't know how he expected me to take care of my own child and three other kids—ages 11, 13 and 16 at the time—with no job. All he said to me was, "You all will be okay."

I wanted to kill myself. Once I digested everything, I put it in my mind that I didn't have a choice and that I had God on my side. I then applied for food stamps and welfare because I was not receiving assistance financially from my baby's father, nor was he around.

Being a first time mother was hard enough even if my younger siblings were well behaved, but they were not. My youngest brother and my sister were constantly getting kicked out of school. When the school requested to speak with a parent, I never showed up because I didn't know what to do. Those two were out of control and they eventually dropped out of school. My sister became pregnant at the age of fourteen. My 16-year-old brother at the time, graduated from school and cut hair for money to provide for himself.

After a year of parenting alone, I received a call from my mother. She asked if she could come stay with us because she was homeless. I told her she could but she would have to respect my house. She agreed that she would but when she moved in, she quickly forgot her vow. She would get drunk, cuss me out and play the stereo as loud as it would go. When she was sober, it felt good having her around because we would laugh and clown. But as far as being a mother, she didn't know how. My youngest brother acted as if he couldn't stand her. He never had too much to say to her. He would listen to me before he would listen to her. I knew in my heart that he was hurt because he'd never bonded with her.

A month after my mom moved in, I received a call from my father. He asked if he could come stay with the kids and me, too. I thought back to all the times when we were little and he did whatever he had to do to make sure we ate and were clothed. He would go to this church where they issued out clothes for the needy, and sold his plasma just to provide us with food. At night he held us in his arms and would tell us how much he loved us while he wept. Even though he struggled with his mental illness, paranoid schizophrenic, I always appreciated all of the sacrifices he made for us. Was I confused, hurt and afraid about my relationship with him? Yes, but I knew I could make it through with the help of my Heavenly Father. So, even though he was suffering with his illness, I could not turn my back on him. I told him; of course he could come and stay.

Having my parents in the house at the same time was odd. Sometimes they would get along and sometimes they wouldn't. He was quiet and she was the complete opposite. Overall, I was relieved because I felt like I had some help around the house.

Throughout everything I was going through I knew that God had my back and was with me at all times. I always loved God and knew that He was real. As I was growing up, I never felt that my childhood was a childhood and that it wasn't fair what I had to endure. However, I knew that God's love made me strong enough to get through it all.

Do you always find yourself sacrificing for others? If so, pray this prayer with me.

Heavenly Father,

Thank You for Your love and affection, and allowing me to make it this far. Thank You for my health and strength and for always being by my side, even when I felt alone. Jesus, thank you for laying your life down for me, because it gave me the strength to lay down my life for others. In Your Name I pray, Amen.

Scriptures

Deuteronomy 31:6

"Be strong and of a good courage, fear not, nor be afraid of them: for the LORD thy God, he it is that doth go with thee; he will not fail thee, nor forsake thee." (KJV)

Psalm 18:32-34

"It is God that girdeth me with strength, and maketh my way perfect. He maketh my feet like hinds' feet, and setteth me upon my high places. He teacheth my hands to war, so that a bow of steel is broken by mine arms." (KJV)

Chapter Four – Patterns

According to Steve Nimmons of *Insights and Analysis,* "Patterns are a consistent and recurring characteristic or trait that helps in the identification of a phenomenon or problem, and serves as an indicator or model for predicting its future behavior."

Once we become adults and start raising our own children, we begin to reflect on our childhood. In reflection we become more understanding of our parent's "mistakes," realizing that most times they were doing their best based off of how they were raised.

One day I asked my father about his childhood. He explained to me that his mother had nine kids and raised all of them on her own. She had given him and a couple of his siblings away to a woman that was mean and hateful. She did indescribable things and whipped them so badly that one day he ran away and never turned back. He grew up without his father and without any guidance. A lot of things that he learned, he learned on his own and survived by the grace of God.

Growing up, my dad never sat my sister and me down and told us about the birds and the bees, as they would say. He never explained to us how a man was supposed to treat a woman. So one of the patterns that was displayed in my life was lack of parenting and nurturing from my grandmother to my father, and now from him to me.

Without proper parental guidance throughout my life, I found myself making a lot of mistakes. Because of my feelings of hurt, abandonment and neglect, I started a behavior that I kept repeating, creating a pattern. As I mentioned, in my teen years, I slept with guys just to fill that void but always ended up back at square one. I felt guilty, dirty, ashamed and unworthy.

When I became pregnant with my first child, I didn't know the challenges that I would face being a mother with no assistance from the father. He was an older guy who lived the fast life. He had no father present in his life, not much education and he was in and out of jail.

But back then, it was something about him that made me happy when he came around even when he didn't provide for, or assist me with our baby. I basically revolved my life around him. I would sit by the phone hoping he would call to see how we were doing. There were many days that I felt heartbroken because of the rejection.

One day he came over to the house for the first time to meet my father. He had his music blasting and the base caused the mirror on our living room wall to vibrate. Living the life that he did, he had a lot of money, drove different cars and wore the best clothes and shoes, at the time.

My dad was angry and I was embarrassed. I thought to myself, *why would he come around here with his music blasting?* My dad immediately called him a gangster. My father was strict but what dad wouldn't feel that way? Eventually, he got to know him and he accepted him even though he was undependable.

Being left to raise a child alone left me angry with my child's father. I can remember times when we talked on the phone I would say something about him not being there for his child, which caused a huge disagreement. One of the things that hurt me the most was that it seemed he spent time and did for his other children. I couldn't understand why he made a difference? He even told people that our baby wasn't his. What I didn't realize is that he didn't know how to be a father, that the devil had him blinded, and most of all, God had a better plan for the both of us.

What we have to realize is that the enemy loves to cause confusion in families and relationships. But, as time went by, I thanked God that this "gangster" wasn't in my son's life because of the life he was living. Today, I can honestly say that I can now have a conversation with him without arguing. I forgave him for not partnering with me in the raising of our son and ultimately had a better understanding of why things had gone the way they had.

In prior relationships I had no reservations about having sex. By the time I met my husband, I realized that sleeping with different guys didn't change or eliminate any of my problems or my hidden hurt, I decided to make him, wait for sex.

As a child, being raised by a single parent was challenging for me. My dad did everything that he could to make sure that our needs were met but he wasn't much of a communicator. When we'd done something wrong, he would yell or even whip us instead of explaining to us what we could've done differently.

I was a single parent at the age of nineteen. I never expected my life to be like this. When I dreamed of one day having a family of my own, I always wanted my children to be raised in a healthy two-parent home, which I'd never experienced. Again, I was repeating the pattern.

As I listened to other people talk about how they communicated with their children, it made me realize that I lacked skills in that area as a parent. After my husband and I were married and had our family, I decided to talk to my children about the dos and don'ts. As I look back, I could've done a better job. Communicating was difficult for me because of what I was hiding on the inside. Sometimes I found myself yelling at my children when they'd done something wrong, instead of talking to them and getting to the root of the problem.

I decided to break the patterns that were destroying my family, including the abandonment issues and the abuse of drugs and alcohol. I promised my children to be there for them the best way that I knew how, and to provide for and protect them. Having God in our lives was also important to me. That was one of the main things that my dad taught us. That was a good pattern that I chose to leave it intact.

One of the things I'd never had, but always wanted, was a great relationship with my siblings. However, each of us lived separate and different lives. Drugs and alcohol played a major part in my family, which caused division. I never expressed to them what I was going through. Instead, I was the one that everyone would call with their problems.

My dad always said that I was a friendly child and that everyone in the neighborhood wanted to play with me. I was that person that loves all types of people, made other children laugh and helped anyone if I could. I drew others to me because, as they explained, I was the life of the party.

Even though I was this "happy go lucky" type of person, I struggled with not having anyone to talk to. Because of that, I started a pattern of accepting unworthy people, both men and women, into my life.

My friends didn't know all of the pain I had endured over the years. Still, I came across to them as being vulnerable, which I was, but I didn't realize it at the time. I just wanted that brother/sister relationship that I'd never had. I told my friends some of my deepest secrets and things that I was going through. In return, they talked about me, shared my business with others, and used the things I'd shared with them against me to make me look bad.

Some of my closest friends even hated the fact that others liked me. So, they would tell lies on me to make me look like this horrible person. Yes, I may have done some of the things that they said, but I was not who they said I was. I felt guilty and angry with myself, for allowing those people to get close to my heart. There were times I would curl up on my sofa and think about all of the things that was said and done to me and cried myself asleep.

I realize that the enemy sent those people into my life to try to destroy and break me down. But the devil is a liar and when his lies are exposed you have to make a decision to separate the truth from the lies.

God allowed me to see who those "friends" really were so I could recognize that I was repeating the same pattern of clinging to unhealthy relationships. He helped me understand that I had to be mindful of the people that I allowed into my life in the future.

Weeding out unhealthy relationships was especially important for me to do before God could show me what He had planned for me. I had to forgive my friends and let them go. I'm not going to lie; because I loved them, letting them go was a hard to do. But it was necessary.

Today, I can honestly say that it doesn't bother me anymore that I had to let go of these friends and they are no longer in my life. I have forgiven them and moved on. Two major lessons I learned on breaking negative patterns in relationships are:

1. Be mindful of the people that you are allowing into your life.
2. Different people have different motives.

I thank the Holy Spirit for that revelation.

If you can name any negative patterns that currently exist in your life, know that it's time to break them for yourself and for the next generations of your family. In order to live a healthier and happier life, we have to do things differently.

Sit down in a quiet place and think about all of the things that you are doing that hinder you, hold you in bondage and are especially not of God. Are you repeating the same pattern that the enemy allowed for so many years to tear you and your family down? If so, what are you going to do about it? If this is difficult for you to do, pray and ask God to show you how. It's time to make a change and live a happier life.

Heavenly Father,

Help me to identify the things that are holding me in bondage and the things that hinder me. Thank You, God for allowing me to notice the patterns that have lingered in my family for years. I pray that the pattern stops here with me. Show me the people that I need to forgive and let go of. Help me to prepare for your best. In Jesus' Name, I pray, Amen.

Scriptures
Psalm 139: 23-24
"Search me, O God, and know my heart: try me, and know my thoughts: And see if *there be any* wicked way in me, and lead me in the way everlasting." (KJV)

1 Corinthians 15:33
Be not deceived: evil communications corrupt good manners." (KJV)

Chapter Five – Breaking Patterns

Watching my mom struggle with alcohol and drug abuse, and not having a place to call her own, made me want more out of life. I didn't want to repeat the same patterns that I'd witnessed in my family. I didn't want that life for my future family and me so I promised myself that when I had kids, I wouldn't abandon them. Even if I had to go without, I would make sure that they always had a safe place to stay, clothes and shoes. I would go to their activities and be an active parent.

When we got home from school as a child, my dad sat us down and helped us with our homework. He went over our spelling words with us and then told us to study so he could give us a spelling test later that night. If we misspelled a word, we'd get a lick with the belt on our hands. I guess that's why I'm a good speller to this day. He was big on education but unfortunately he never enforced the importance of us going to college.

In high school I would hear the other students talk about going to college, so that made me want to go to better myself. Even though I didn't have a clue to what I was doing, I decided to fill out an application to a local college, Southern University of New Orleans. I even filled out my own financial aid application. But it was months after graduating from high school that I found out that I was pregnant. I was happy, but disappointed at the same time because of the things that I had planned.

After completing my first semester, I didn't go back because I had a new baby and was forced to raise my siblings. Not finishing college, I found myself struggling to get the job that I really wanted because it required a degree. So, I promised myself that I would teach my children the importance of receiving a college education. Today, that is exactly what my husband and I emphasize. Our oldest son has a degree in Psychology and we are so proud of his achievements. He's the first one in my immediate family that received a college education. I told him before and after his graduation that I was proud of him for breaking that cycle and starting a new one.

Making the decision to break a pattern in your family takes hard work and commitment. When I decided to walk away from my family, I was excited, but afraid at the same time. I wondered if I could handle all of my bills and still be able to survive. Being on Section Eight, I didn't have to pay any rent and I got a utility check for about $90 to help me with my utility bill. Even though it was a struggle, my happiness was more important, so I was willing to take that chance and trust in God, just to be happy.

After moving on my own, I was still receiving a small amount in food stamps but it was enough to help me provide food for my child. Yes, being on Section 8, welfare, childcare assistance and food stamps was helpful, but I knew in my heart that I didn't want to live on the system for the rest of my life.

My entire life I'd witnessed the enemy destroy my family with drugs and alcohol. I'd also watched how it affected my generation in such a negative way. Some of my relatives suffered with drug and alcohol abuse that began because of the anger and hate in their hearts towards their parents. Other relatives abused alcohol and drugs because of their upbringing and watching their parents do drugs in front of them. Others were dealing with low self-esteem or they dropped out of school at such a young age and went into that lifestyle. Watching their parents use drugs led others in my generation to develop patterns of overeating, unhealthy living, looking for love through sex and even death.

One day when my brother was in his early 20s, he called me furious, and speaking very irrationally. He was angry that our father had not provided him with a normal life and proper education. He even mentioned that he could've put us in private school. He was comparing our life to white people. He said, "White people make sure that their kids finish school and prepare them for college." He went on and on. His frustration was surrounded by the fact that he had been trying to find a job, but couldn't because of his lack of education. What I realized is that he was hurting and had never expressed it until that day. I explained to him that our father had done the best he could. He'd done only what he knew how to do.

I told my brother that living the life that we lived should make him want to do better for himself and his future kids. If he wanted a better job, I suggested that he go get his GED. He wasn't trying to hear anything I said.

My brother began to drink a lot. And not only was he smoking weed, he was even selling it. He'd started hanging around the wrong people and was doing the wrong things. I would drill into him over and over again how dangerous this lifestyle was but couldn't get through to him. What I didn't know was he was as angry with me as well as our father.

My brother was angry all of his life. He acted on that anger by making poor choices and living a hard, fast and violent life. He had three instances of gun violence. The first was when he was shot multiple times by his supervisor while on the job. The second instance happened when he was sitting on the porch of a friend when someone tried to shoot him in the head but grazed his neck. The third instance would be the last. In 2008 he was shot in the back of the head and died from the gunshot wound.

Suddenly, I was left with only two siblings. They both struggled with alcohol and drug addictions, which led to less than productive lives. My middle brother was in and out of jail. He's now serving an 8-year sentence on possession of drug paraphernalia while on parole. Before he went to jail, he and my youngest brother got into a heated argument and weren't speaking when my youngest brother was killed.

At my youngest brother's funeral, my middle brother was wearing prison clothes, handcuffs and shackles. As I watched him, he cried continuously through the service. I remembered telling him to make peace with his little brother because anything could happen. He wasn't trying to hear anything that I was saying. Then, it was too late.

My sister has struggled with her addiction her entire adult life thus far. She dropped out of school at an early age, and to this day, she doesn't have much education. For years she lived with the hurt that she buried deep down inside. She had two kids and raised them to the best of her ability. She made sure that her kids ate and had clothes until her addictions took over.

She drank heavily and did drugs while neglecting her kids and home. Her addiction got so bad that she ended up homeless and my husband and I cared for her 14-year-old son. Even though her current situation still looks bad, I thank God in advance for her deliverance and for Him transforming her mind, and most of all, saving her.

One day my youngest son came home from school and gave me a kiss on the cheek. He was 15-years-old at the time. When he leaned towards me, I picked up a marijuana scent. I jumped up and accused him of smoking weed but he vehemently denied it. I yelled at him to tell the truth but he insisted that he wasn't lying.

The only thing that I remember was hitting him until my hands went numb. He finally admitted that he had smoked it and that it was his first time trying it. I know that it was God that brought it to my attention because what person with common sense would kiss their parents after smoking a joint?

After collecting myself, I sat him down to explain how drugs could affect not just him, but the whole family. I told him how it affected your body, appearance, career and actions. He cried and said he wouldn't do it again. I knew that my son was under attack by the enemy. The devil had plans to continue that drug and alcohol addiction pattern that affected my entire family. I prayed and rebuked the devil and his demons, immediately.

As I continued to pray, my son continued getting in trouble. He had problems at school; he was hanging with the wrong people and still smoking marijuana. Until one Friday afternoon, I received a call from the school letting me know that he was being arrested for possession of marijuana on the campus. I was devastated.

He had to sit in the county jail until Tuesday because Monday was a holiday. Words couldn't explain the way I felt, but I knew that God was dealing with him and teaching him a lesson. Because of the crime that he had committed, he was looking at time in juvenile detention. I prayed that God showed him favor through the judge.

When it was time for him to go before the judge, I was nervous. While looking over his eyeglasses, the judge asked him several questions. My heart was literally about to jump out of my chest. I hoped my son said the right things and responded with respect by saying, 'yes sir' and 'no sir' when needed. The judge told him that he could tell that he was respectful, had potential and that he had great parents. He gave him a 6-month probation sentence and told him he'd be tested every week. He also told him that if all of the test results were negative, and he stayed out of trouble, he'd have a clean record.

When the judge said that I felt the weight lift off of my shoulders and I thanked God immediately. Ultimately, he completed probation with flying colors and had a clean record. God was good.

All was well, or so I thought. Two years later in the summer of 2014, after arriving home from work, I went to the laundry room to start my laundry. I smelled cigarette smoke on my son's dirty clothes. He was now 17-years old and out with friends so I called him on his cell phone and told him to come home. Without me saying anything more, I could tell by his response he knew why I was calling.

When he arrived home he said, "Momma, it looks like the dryer was trying to catch a fire, I saw smoke coming from underneath it. I had all of my clothes in the dryer and now they smell like cigarettes."

I accused him of lying and gave him another chance to tell the truth. He stuck to his story until I took his phone and punished him.

After expressing how I felt, I walked every room in my home and shouted, "Devil, I rebuke you and every demonic force that's trying to take over my family. You and your demons been in my family for years causing all kinds of problems, but this generational curse stops here. You can't have my children. My family is delivered from drugs and alcohol. You and your demons have to flee! Get out of my house, in the name of Jesus!"

My son looked at me like I was crazy. I was yelling so loudly, my throat hurt and I felt dizzy. War was crazy but victory was sweet. And I know that God gave me the victory of saved, drug-free children.

One day in September 2014, I woke up curious about my son's health and drug status so I had my husband make him a doctor's appointment. I had him tested for all STD's and for drug use. He had no idea why his father was taking him to the doctor until he arrived there. I was working and anxiously awaiting the results. My husband was taking too long to call me so I called him. That's when he told me that they were going to call us or mail us the results.

After not hearing from them for a week, I assumed that everything was okay. And one day in the mailbox an envelope from the doctor's office arrived. I couldn't open it fast enough. All STD's results were negative and he was negative for all drugs. That was a sigh of relief for me. I couldn't thank God enough.

I spoke with a close friend recently and he told me that he and several of his family members, had been molested by his Aunt Laura. I looked at the pattern. I told him that his Aunt Laura had most likely been sexually abused herself. He said he actually knew she had been by another relative. He also stated that he'd hated her for years for what she had done to him, but eventually forgave her. As far as his father, who had also been one of her victims, he turned to drugs and was currently living with a terminal disease. His brother turned to drugs and was living his life full of anger and un-forgiveness in his heart. As far as the other family members, they were all drug and alcohol abusers. Look at the pattern.

How do we identify a pattern? Go back as far as you can go in your family tree and identify the recurring characteristics or traits that have been lingering in your family for years. Look at all of the people that it has affected in a negative way.

Do you want your children to repeat the pattern? What can you do to stop it? If you look at the tile on your floor, it has a pattern that the contractor followed to lay it down. It connects up, down and side-to-side, but comes to an end at some point. Will that be you?

First, you must pray and ask The Holy Spirit to reveal the patterns present in your family. Once He shows you, you must decide if you want to break the generational curse that the devil orchestrated to destroy you and your family. Change is going to be necessary.

When my dad was diagnosed with Paranoid Schizophrenia, it explained a lot about his behavior when I was a child. I've learned now that it's deeper than a mental diagnosis but is also spiritual. My father was dealing with demonic forces that had been trying to take him out for years. My family had been under attack since I was born, and I'm quite sure, even before that. Yes, the devil was successful with some of my family members, but as long as I had breath in my body, I would stand boldly for my family and me. The pattern stops here, IN THE NAME OF JESUS!

My friend Larry was a great dad and wanted to have the best relationship a father and daughter could have. He provided child support but wasn't able to see his daughter the way he desired. Samantha would tell her daughter bad things about him and spoke negative things to others while their daughter listened. If she were angry with Larry, she wouldn't let him see his child until she was ready. Sadly, she had another daughter whose father wasn't present in her life at all.

One day Larry and Samantha had a disagreement. She told Larry she'd never had her own father present in her life, so she didn't think that her children needed their fathers in their life either. "Look how I turned out!" she boasted.

Larry couldn't believe what he was hearing. Samantha was a broken woman who brought plenty of men around her daughters. She didn't understand how important it is to have a father around. She didn't realize that not having her father around played a major role in how she treated her children's fathers and the choices that she had made. Larry fought with Samantha for years about spending time with his daughter and never had the relationship that he wanted—the relationship that a father and daughter should have. He would get jealous when he heard his friends talk about their daughters and was deeply saddened by being robbed of that opportunity.

Today Larry's daughter, Connie, is now a mother. She doesn't allow the father to bond with their baby like a father should, either. If he wants to visit the baby, he has to go to their home and is not allowed to take the baby. If Connie is mad with him, he's lucky if he's able to see the baby at all. The only thing that is important to Connie is the money given from the child's father.

Both, Connie and her mother, pushed great fathers away from their children because of their selfishness and controlling behavior. What Connie doesn't realize is that she is repeating the same pattern that her mom started. Connie is broken, hurt, and lonely and still allows her mom to control her. When will it ever end? Will her baby continue the pattern or break it? Only time will tell.

Once you have realized the patterns that are in your life, and have broken them, you may start to see patterns in the lives of the people around you. While it is always right to care for others, it is difficult to help someone who doesn't want to be free. Patterns are not always visible to the person woven into the lifestyle. Prayers are needed and much patience if you have a loved one who is in a pattern that they cannot see. You can help them become naked by lovingly sharing with them what you see and helping them peel off the layers of dysfunction. In the meantime, let's pray for your family's patterns to be broken.

Heavenly Father,

I ask in the Name of Jesus that you break every curse that has been affecting my family for generations. I pray that You give me the strength and the will power to stand boldly against those patterns that are placed in my family's life by the enemy to destroy us. Give me the words of wisdom and knowledge to pray for them and to share with them. I pray that no weapons formed against my family will prosper. I rebuke the devil and all of the things that he has used to devour us. God, I know that You're able to do abundantly more than what we ask for. I am thanking You in advance for deliverance in my family's life. In Jesus' Name I pray, Amen!

Scriptures
Deuteronomy 28:1-7
"And it shall come to pass, if thou shalt hearken diligently unto the voice of the Lord thy God, to observe and to do all his commandments which I command thee this day, that the Lord thy God will set thee on high above all nations of the earth: And all these blessings shall come on thee, and overtake thee, if thou shalt hearken unto the voice of the Lord thy God. Blessed shalt thy be in the city, and blessed shalt thy be in the field. Blessed shall be the fruit of thy body, and the fruit of thy ground, and the fruit of thy cattle, the increase of thy kine, and the flocks of thy sheep. Blessed shall be thy basket and thy store. Blessed shall thy be when thou comest in, and blessed shalt thou be when thou goest out. The Lord shall cause thine enemies that rise up against thee to be smitten before thy face: they shall come out against thee one way, and flee before thee seven ways." (KJV)

Chapter Six – New Beginning

When I turned 21, my life shifted. Being a single mom with no assistance from the baby's father, and all of the chaos going on in my home, I felt like I was going crazy. I had a high school education and was working at the Marriott as a PBX operator. I was the only one working, making $5.35 an hour. Things were tight. As I looked around, everyone seemed to be happy, but me. At the time I was working the mid-day shift, 4:00-12:30 A.M.

Every day I caught the bus and walked home down a quiet street. I just wanted a little peace and some sleep once I got home. My mother would be up drunk and playing the blues as loud as it would go. If I asked her to turn down Muddy Waters, she would call me all kinds of profane names and tell me she wouldn't. Everyone in the house would be upset because they couldn't sleep. She would come to my room and start an argument and sometimes try to fight me.

One day in particular she tried to spit in my face but it went in my hair. Lord knows I wanted to slap her as hard as I could, but I couldn't do it. I was so upset I called the police and had her removed from the house. I had every intention of letting her back in but I wanted her to learn a lesson. After about an hour or two she started knocking on my window pleading for me to let her back in. Eventually, I did let her in, explaining to her that it was my house and she was going to obey my rules. When she entered, she was quiet as a mouse and got her blanket, tiptoed to the sofa and went to sleep.

Most days after arriving home from work, the house would be filthy. My bills were past due and I had no one to assist me. I wanted a way out but I couldn't figure out how to do it without hurting my family. I was providing food and shelter for my mother, father, sister and my sister's daughter, in addition to my two brothers and my own son. And because I knew that all seven of them depended on me, leaving them was a tough decision to make. When I decided to leave them all, my little brother later told me that he felt like he had been abandoned all over again. I didn't realize when I left them it left a hole in his heart. That explained why he stopped speaking to me.

It seemed like no one was getting along. My dad was the only quiet one. He wouldn't bother anyone. The house was always noisy with people running in and out. As time went by, I couldn't take the stress anymore so I grabbed the telephone book and searched all of the homeless shelters nearby. I was crying so much I couldn't see anything on the pages.

Most of the shelters wanted to take your paycheck and place it in an account and would only give me an allowance. After calling on particular one, I was told that there was only one bathroom and one kitchen that all of the families shared. I said to myself, *oh no, I can't do that one.* I was particular about certain things, so I knew that wouldn't work for me, especially sitting on a toilet behind all of those different people. I thought about one of my coworkers who was once homeless, so I called her for advice.

She agreed that a shelter wouldn't be a good idea for me and my son. She told me she had just moved into a one-bedroom apartment and there was more available, giving me the landlord's number.

I immediately called Mr. Green. He said that he had only one apartment available, ready to be moved in, and that the rent was two hundred and seventy five dollars with a $275 deposit. He let me move in with first month's rent and let me make payments on the deposit.

I was so happy I couldn't compose myself. Not to mention, I was terrified that I didn't know what I was getting myself into. I didn't know the condition of the apartment, but it didn't matter at the time. I just wanted out.

After telling my family that I was leaving and moving into my own place, the first thing my siblings said was, "What are we going to do? Who will pay the bills? Why are you leaving us?"

I said to them, "I don't know! Dad can put the lights in his name and you all will find a way to pay the bills. And I'm giving the Section 8 voucher back to Dad."

My mother and my youngest brother stopped speaking to me for a while. My father was happy for me. He got a job as a stockman at a grocery store and was able to let me borrow $65 to get my water turned on. Things were going to be tight but I was willing to do what I had to for my baby and myself.

When it was time to meet with the landlord, I had butterflies. I didn't know what to expect. I arrived and saw this old large white two-story house, which required a key to get through the gate. It had large, long windows in the front and a doorway leading to some stairs in the hallway. I thought to myself, *I think I'm going to like this.* When he arrived, he was a tall old man with light brown skin and gray hair. He was very polite and nice.

As we walked through the gate, we made a left and went to the side of the house. There were two entrances with iron bars on each, separated by two large windows with shutters. When I entered the apartment I was so impressed.

I entered and saw a large brick fireplace, but without the pit. It had a heater that sat under the brick mantle. There was an all-brick wall separating my apartment from the other apartment. The living room and the kitchen were combined in one large, open area. It came with one bedroom and one bathroom. It was perfect for my son and me. I gave him my first month's rent and he gave me my keys. That was one of the happiest moments of my life. I felt free and I couldn't thank God enough for blessing us!

When I moved in, the only things I had were a bedroom set, a used refrigerator I'd purchased from a salvage store, a few pots and pans and a 19-inch television. Months later, my grandfather blessed me with his old sofa with a built in recliner. A coworker gave me a table that he'd built, but with no chairs. I was happy with both the sofa and table because it made my apartment look fully furnished and it was better than what I'd had before. I was so appreciative. It seemed like once God started blessing me, He never stopped. I felt a sense of peace and like my life was just beginning.

One day while sitting in the cafeteria eating breakfast before I started my shift, I noticed this guy staring at me the whole time while I ate. He was tall—about six-foot three-inch—brown skin with a mustache, short wavy hair, thick neck and a very nice body. I tried to act as if I didn't notice him staring, but I couldn't help but to stare back. We never said a word to each other and I was hoping to see him the next day. We saw each other every morning around the same time, as if it were planned.

One day he invited me to his table to sit and have breakfast with him. I was so nervous to eat in front of him that I acted as if I were full and I didn't finish my food. My stomach was growling. Basically, my stomach was touching my back.

We had a nice conversation and talked about our children. I asked him why he'd stared at me. That's when he told me he thought I was a beautiful woman. I thought to myself, *you're not too bad looking yourself.* But, I said aloud, "Well, thank you!" I was flattered but didn't want to show it.

Throughout my life I wasn't told that I was pretty so it felt good coming from him. After breakfast, we both went to our respective work areas. Later that day I ran into my cousin who worked in the parking garage of the hotel. When I looked to the right, I spotted this tall handsome stallion. When he turned around, I noticed it was the same guy from breakfast.

I asked my cousin if he worked with him. He said, "Who, Jude? Yes, he works with me. Why, are you interested in him?" I told my cousin that Jude seemed like a nice guy and to have him to call me on my office phone.

Every time the phone rang, I thought it was Jude calling. Well, he took a little too long so I called him. We talked for a brief minute, exchanging home phone numbers and talked on the phone almost every day. I couldn't put my finger on it but there was something special about him.

About a week later he came to my office to tell me that he was offered a new job working on a cruise boat that would require him to be gone for six weeks at a time. I was disheartened. I thought, *well, I know this isn't going any further*. He asked me to write down my name and address so that he could write me while he was away.

After not hearing from him, I basically wrote him off. One day I received a letter and was surprised and excited to read what he had to say. I mean this wasn't a one-paragraph letter. It was about two pages long, and he had the nerve to draw a beautiful colored rose on the bottom of the letter. There was one thing that caught my attention at the end of the letter when he wrote, "Tell my boy Travis that I said, hello." I couldn't figure out who Travis was. Maybe, he had me mixed up with another woman. That left me puzzled and ticked off. Every day when I got home, I would run to the mailbox just to see if I'd received another letter from him. He wrote me on a constant basis and always asked about Travis.

One day I received a collect call from him. I was excited, but I was curious about how much it was going to cost. I couldn't afford to pay for any collect calls. When the call went through, he explained to me that the calls were expensive and that he was going to pay me for it.

As we talked, I finally got to ask him who Travis was. All that time he was asking about my son. When I told him my son's name was Kentrell, we laughed hysterically. He said, "I don't know why I thought you said his name was Travis."

Jude mentioned that he was coming home soon and that he wanted to see me. Everything seemed surreal because I thought that once he left, he would forget about me. His first day back home he came over to visit my son and me. As he walked towards me I didn't think he looked like the same guy that I'd first met. He had a short Afro and a face full of hair and it wasn't appealing to me at all.

When I asked him about his mini Afro and beard, he said he was anxious to see me first but planned to get a haircut and shave later. Even though he looked like a grizzly bear, he had earned a point. Bells were ringing in my head.

With him being home for only two weeks, he spent a lot of time with me. One day he came over to hang out with my son and me and while he sat on the sofa, for some reason, he couldn't keep still and had this strange look on his face. He finally asked if he could use my bathroom. He looked at me and said, "I have to do number two."

He got up and shot to the bathroom. I looked at him and turned my nose up. I was turned off when I smelled the odor coming from the bathroom. I wanted to light incense but I didn't want to insult him. I didn't understand why he didn't wait until he got home.

When he returned to the living room, he had the nerve to ask me, "Did I have any incense?" I thought to myself, *No he didn't!* On the one hand I was thinking the same thing but I was surprised that he had the nerve to ask without shame.

As time went by, Jude became more and more attractive to me. I had made up my mind that I didn't want to rush into having sex. I didn't want to make the same mistakes that I'd made in the past. And, I wanted him to like me for the person that I was and also have respect for me.

One day my family was having a picnic and I invited him to come. Before going to the picnic, he asked if we could stop by his mother's home because he wanted to introduce me. That's when I knew he was serious about me.

Jude's mom told me that he had a lot of wonderful things to say about me. That caught me by surprise because I didn't know that he saw anything wonderful about me or felt the way that he did. That was another brownie point for him.

Normally I would go to family gatherings alone. So, when we arrived at the picnic, I was ecstatic about introducing him to the family. Later, we took a stroll around the park. We held hands, laughed and talked. I never had anyone to treat me the way that he had. In my heart I knew that we were going to be more than friends.

That evening we became intimate. Being with him was different from the other guys I had been with. I felt such an unexplainable connection. I couldn't get him off of my mind. When it was time for him to leave to go back to work for six weeks, I was sad.

I invited Jude to go on a trip to AstroWorld in Houston with my cousin and her boyfriend. At first I was reluctant because I knew I couldn't afford it. But he assured me he was paying for everything.

While we were on the trip we were able to learn more about each other. We had such a great time and words couldn't explain how I was feeling about him. I was afraid to show or express how I felt because I was so used to getting my heart broken, and I didn't want it to happen again.

Once we returned, he stayed over at my house and was basically living out of his suitcase. When he needed more clothes, he would go home and get some little by little. Before we knew it, all of his clothes were in my closet. I told him if he wanted to stay, he could if he wanted. From that day forward, we were living together. Shacking up is what it's really called.

I was always an independent person and had never asked anyone to help me with my bills. But when Jude saw me sitting on the bed balancing my checkbook and paying bills, he asked what the monthly expenses were. I told him what I paid and he said he would pay the rent and I could pay the rest of the bills. I couldn't believe what I was hearing.

I was so excited that I thought the world was coming to an end. With him contributing, I was able to buy things that I hadn't been able to buy before. I knew it was a blessing from God and I couldn't thank God enough!

Out of nowhere one day, while riding in the car my son called Jude, Daddy. I was embarrassed and was wondering how it made him feel. I immediately said, "That's not your daddy!" Kentrell said, "Yes it is!" He said it with enthusiasm and a big smile on his face.

When I looked at Jude, he had a look on his face as if he was puzzled. As time went by he spent a lot of time with Kentrell. When he picked up his daughter, he would do different activities with both of the children. He always included him and that meant a lot to me because my son had never had a father figure.

One day Jude suggested that we needed a bigger place. He said that Kentrell needed his own room and we needed our privacy. He said he was willing to pay $400-$500. I couldn't believe he was willing to pay that kind of money for rent for us. In 1996, that was a lot.

We started looking immediately and eventually found a beautiful two-bedroom town home with, one and a half bath, a living room and a nook area. We purchased new furniture, which we paid on monthly. I didn't realize that I was blessed with a gift in decorating. If I had known life could be this wonderful, I would've left home a long time ago. Again, I knew it was God's doing.

I felt like I'd never felt before. I knew in my heart that Jude was going to be by husband one day and I told him that. He told me he wasn't thinking about marriage. I respected what he said, but still, I knew we would be married. When I insisted that he was going to be my husband, he just chuckled.

We spent a lot of time together as a family. We went on family outings to Chuck E. Cheese, the movies, skating, etc. Life really started looking good to me. Being able to come home from work to a quiet and well-furnished house felt great.

I knew that Jude had all of the potential to be a husband, but he needed to make some changes in different areas of his life. He didn't have his own father in his life to teach him how to be a man, but I was impressed with how he treated me and handled different situations. I was more mature than he was but the things that he didn't know, I could teach him. He made my heart smile with the love that he was giving my son and me. It made me want to treat him like a king.

I kept a clean home and made sure he had a hot meal when he came home. And I made sure that our intimacy was on point. All of this was new to me because I didn't grow up with parents who did those things for each other. It was something that seemed to come naturally, so I just followed my instincts.

In all of my past relationships I walked away with a broken heart, but I was willing to give him a chance to love me the way I'd always wanted to be loved. I didn't trust men in general, and was carrying a lot of baggage, but I didn't want to show it because I didn't want to run him off.

Having a partner by your side that's going to have your back at all times was important. Feeling loved is one of the greatest feelings in the world. I was grateful for my new beginning because it led me into the arms of someone who loved me and treated me right. We were a team and I loved how it felt to win. Our relationship made the distant past a blur and I was so full of love for him that you couldn't tell me that our bliss wouldn't last forever. However, it didn't.

Are you ready to close some unhealthy doors and let God lead you to new ones? If so, pray this prayer with me.

Heavenly Father,

Thank you for allowing me to show love to my family in spite of all of the challenges that are placed before me. Thank You for being by my side when I decided to leap out on my own, and for supplying all of my needs. Thank You for brand new mercies every morning and your unconditional love. In Jesus' Name I pray, Amen.

Scriptures
1 Corinthians 13: 1-13

"Though I speak with the tongues of men and of angels, and have not charity, I am become as sounding brass, or a tinkling cymbal. And though I have the gift of prophecy, and understand all mysteries, and all knowledge; and though I have all faith, so that I could remove mountains, and have not charity, I am nothing. And though I bestow all my goods to feed the poor, and though I give my body to be burned, and have not charity, it profiteth me nothing. Charity suffereth long, and is kind; charity envieth not; charity vaunteth not itself, is not puffed up, Doth not behave itself unseemly, seeketh not her own, is not easily provoked, thinketh no evil; Rejoiceth not in iniquity, but rejoiceth in the truth; Beareth all things, believeth all things, hopeth all things, endureth all things.

Charity never faileth: but whether there be prophecies, they shall fail; whether there be tongues, they shall cease; whether there be knowledge, it shall vanish away. For we know in part, and we prophesy in part. But when that which is perfect is come, then that which is in part shall be done away. When I was a child, I spake as a child, I understood as a child, I thought as a child: but when I became a man, I put away childish things. For now we see through a glass, darkly; but then face to face: now I know in part; but then shall I know even as also I am known.

And now abideth faith, hope, charity, these three; but the greatest of these is charity." (KJV)

Chapter Seven – When Getting it Right Goes Wrong

At the age of 24 God began dealing with me about the way I was living. After shacking up for a little over a year, the spirit of conviction weighed heavy on my heart. I thought to myself, *if I'm good enough to live with, I'm good enough to marry.* I knew I needed to talk to Jude and express exactly how I felt.

One day Jude called home from work to check on Kentell and me. I told him I had something important to talk to him about. I had some reservations about the way we were living. We were having sex outside of wedlock and that it was not right. I told him that I wasn't trying to force him into something that he wasn't ready for, but he had until the end of the year to propose to me.

He asked, "So, what if I I'm not ready to be married? If we don't get married, then what will happen?"

I told him if he wasn't ready, I couldn't force him to be but we were going to have to move into separate households and do things differently. We could still date but I wanted to start living right. He said he understood.

I wondered what was going to happen next and I didn't have to wait long. Some months later I sat at my desk at work and realized that I couldn't remember having my cycle. I decided to go to the drug store on my lunch break to buy a pregnancy test. I called two of my girlfriends and asked if they could meet me in the restroom because I didn't want to be alone while I took the test. The test recommended that I wait a full five minutes for the results and that was the longest five minutes of my life. When it was time to read the results, my heart began to palpitate. The test results were positive. I was so excited, but was curious about how Jude would feel. I couldn't wait until he called home so I could share the good news.

Jude was still working out of town and after a few days passed, he finally called. After I broke the news, he said he hoped it was a boy. I could hear the excitement in his voice. I was hoping for a girl. The addition to our family was exciting and I could see big things happening soon in our lives.

I was so happy that I felt like I was walking on cloud nine. Being with him each and every day gave me butterflies, as if we had just met. We had many special moments as a couple. We made a pallet on the floor, popped popcorn, drank ice-cold glasses of Coca-Cola, cuddled up and watched a movie. Jude did romantic things such as: run my bath water and sprinkled rose petals on top; prepared candlelight dinners with flowers. He surprised me with the things that I loved most such as, chocolate, perfume and taking me to nice restaurants. That was living the life to me. I didn't have to run the streets nor did I feel the need to have plenty of friends around. Besides God, I felt like having him was all that I needed.

One day Jude and I decided to go to dinner and a movie. I felt like something was going on but I couldn't put my finger on it. He was acting super nice and anxious. When we got in the car, he said, "I'll be right back." I was wondering why he went back inside the house. After returning from the movies, he let me go into the bedroom first. When I entered, the lights were dimmed with a pillow sitting in the middle of the bed. At that time I didn't have on my eyeglasses or my contacts, so I couldn't make out what was sitting on the pillow. Once I got closer, I saw a beautiful ring with baguettes surrounding it, sitting in a black box. I turned to him with my hands over my mouth in disbelief. I had the biggest smile on my face.

He looked me in the eyes and said, "Will you marry me?"

Of course, I said. "YES!" So now, I'm pregnant and engaged to the man of my dreams. Things were going pretty good and I was on cloud nine.

In my fourth month of my pregnancy, Jude picked me up from work one day. He seemed to be a little disturbed, but I didn't say anything. Once we were almost to the house he said nervously, "Romella, I have something that I want to tell you. This morning I called one of my exes on the house phone by accident. I am letting you know because she may call back later." When I asked him what ex-girlfriend he was talking about, he said that it was someone he was involved with years ago.

I knew in my heart that he wasn't telling me the whole truth. My heart beat uncontrollably and I literally wanted to slap him across his face. I fussed and cussed all of the way to the house. When we arrived, I checked my answering machine to see if she'd left any messages. And of course, she had. I couldn't believe what I was hearing. She'd left her name with a call back number. My heart felt like it was in my stomach. I felt sick and started crying. Once I collected myself, I called her. I politely introduced myself, and she was polite as well.

As the two of us talked, she told me that she and Jude had been together sexually the previous weekend. She even described the clothes that he wore from head to toe. She said she knew nothing about me and told me that they were engaged.

How can he be planning to marry her, when he is planning to marry me?"

At the time, he was lying across the bed when I asked him, "Are the two of you engaged?" I immediately put her on speakerphone so she could hear his response.

He denied it saying, years ago he'd given her a cheap ring, but insisted he never proposed to her. She said through the speaker, "Jude, tell her we were together last weekend."

Jude denied it but I knew she was telling the truth. That particular day he and I had an argument and he didn't come home until the next day. He said he had stayed the night over to his mom's house. I remembered when I picked him up from his mother's, he had scratches all over his back. He explained that he'd scratched himself washing his back. I knew he was lying.

I don't think he realized how that affected me, especially while being pregnant. I felt alone all over again, and all of my happiness turned into sadness.

Once she hung up the phone, I was angry and started crying. I looked around and found a full can of starch. I picked it up and threw it at him with all of the strength that I had in body while he was lying across the bed. When he realized that it was headed towards his head, he raised his hand to block it. All of a sudden, blood started gushing out of his arm. I was so angry and hurt that I really didn't care.

He accused me of trying to kill him. I said to him, "I should've!" Then I said, "I got something else for you." I ran down stairs to get a butcher knife. Lord knows I was only bluffing. I wanted him to think that I was going to cut him but when he saw the knife in my hand, he calmly said, "Romella, if you cut me with that knife, I'm going to take it and cut you back." I turned my butt around, went downstairs, placed the knife back in the drawer and sat my tail down.

When he had the nerve to tell me that he had been bleeding for hours and needed to go to the hospital, I told him I wished he'd bleed to death. I know that was harsh, but I was hurt and angry. I couldn't believe that he'd put the baby and me at risk of AIDS or an STD. That left me devastated.

The next day he was scheduled to return to work for six weeks. When he left, I was brokenhearted and full of unanswered questions. I couldn't sleep, eat or function at work nor concentrate on our child. I kept thinking about the scratches on his back. Anger and un-forgiveness built up in my heart. My mind was going in circles. I didn't know if I was coming or going and the trust I had for him was gone. I didn't feel attractive or worthy. Being pregnant by him wasn't exciting anymore. I was back to square one.

Can you identify with being betrayed by the one that you thought would never betray you? If so, pray this prayer with me.

Heavenly Father,

This hurts. I don't know which way to turn but I am asking You to take this pain away from me. It is too familiar and I want to only remember Your faithfulness. Heal my heart in the name of Jesus, Amen.

Scriptures
Psalms 147:3

"He healeth the broken in heart, and bindeth up their wounds."
(KJV)

John 14:27
"Peace I leave with you, my peace I give unto you: not as the
world giveth, give I unto you. Let not your heart be troubled,
neither let it be afraid." (KJV)

Chapter Eight – Back to Square One

It was difficult for me to cope with the hurt and the pain of the betrayal of my fiancé, especially because the situation wasn't resolved before he left for another six weeks to work. The trust in our relationship at this point was non-existent. I would stay up all hours of the night wondering, *what is he doing? Who is he with?*

Was he thinking about how he'd hurt me? Was he hurting for hurting me? Did he care about how this may have affected the baby and me? And mainly, I thought about if and how he had satisfied another woman physically and emotionally. I certainly couldn't help but think about those scratches that were on his back. I knew that I had to get myself together because I didn't want to lose the baby. *What do I do now? Should I leave him? Should I forgive him and stay?* Man, words couldn't explain how I felt.

When he first called home from work the conversation was awkward. He was still denying the affair, which made me even angrier. The questions that I wanted answers to were: *Why? Was there something wrong with me? Did he no longer find me attractive?* I was confused because I knew I'd treated him like a man should be treated. *What did I do wrong?* All of the trust that I had for him was gone out of the window.

When he came home for the first time after all of the shenanigans, it was difficult for me. Every time he would leave the house, I would have negative thoughts. I called him a million times asking, "Where are you? What are you doing? When are you coming home? Who are you with?" While asking all those questions, I listened to what was going on in the background. It was exhausting. I could tell in his voice that he was aggravated but I didn't care. When he got home later that night, I couldn't help but to secretly check for more scratches on his back. This routine went on for a long time.

As time went by and our son was born, things got better, but it didn't change the fact that I didn't trust him anymore. The reason I stayed was because I loved him and I was also afraid of being alone again. But, I wondered how I was going to get through this and if I was ever going to trust him again.

In June 1997, Jude called and told me that he was going to be home in three weeks and wanted to marry me when he came. He said I should do whatever I had to do to plan the wedding. I couldn't believe he was serious. He suggested that we have a small wedding at his mom's house. I told him I'd take care of everything. I was so surprised and excited.

On July 5, 1997 I became Mrs. Jude S. Vaughn, Sr., which was one of the happiest days of my life. After all of the things that had taken place in our relationship, I had serious doubts whether or not we would still marry. With a husband, two boys and a daughter from his previous relationship, would things be different now? Would he ever really grow up? Did he learn his lesson?

Throughout the years, things weren't as perfect as they seemed to others. The infidelity continued, which pushed me further away from him emotionally. Even though I decided to stay, the feelings weren't the same as they were when we first met. When it was time to have sex, my heart and emotions weren't in it at all. Sometimes while having sex with him, it felt like a stranger was raping me. I would say to myself, *I hope he hurries up and get off of me.* I sometimes wondered how I was ever going to get past this.

I literally lost respect for Jude after all of the things that he had taken me through. Being faithful, or being that perfect wife, didn't matter to me anymore. I felt like I had done everything I could possibly do to save my marriage; went to counseling, anointed him, and everything he touched, with holy oil. I prayed, had family members praying and expressed to him how he made me feel and how it affected me.

Jude was numb to my crying. It seemed like my tears meant nothing to him. I believed that I wasn't pretty, sexy or worthy anymore. So, I changed my appearance. My hair was long and beautiful. I cut it all off and changed the color, changed the color of my eyes to grey, lost all of that baby weight and even changed the way I dressed. I thought that if I did all of those things, he would see me and only me. But, of course he didn't.

A year into the marriage, I decided to do something's that I never thought I would ever do in my marriage. I started a friendship with another man and as our friendship developed, I found comfort in that relationship.

It all started one day while working, I met this attractive man. We exchanged phone numbers and communicated frequently. Every day I looked forward to talking to him. He literally made my day and just hearing his voice made me feel attractive again, and helped me get past my hurt and pain, temporarily. Eventually, after talking to him almost daily, I realized that I was beginning to care a lot about him. I found myself thinking about him while sitting next to my husband.

My relations with the other man progressed to another level and we became intimate. I knew in my heart that what I was doing was wrong, but being right didn't matter to me anymore because I felt like, Jude had his fun, why can't I have some fun, too?

Being intimate with the other man wasn't the most important thing to me; it was the attention he showed me: his touch, the jokes we shared together and the sweet words he spoke. At that time he was filling a void inside me, and it felt great. I knew at some point and time, things had to end. The spirit of conviction and guilt were deep in my heart. There were times when I lost sleep feeling guilty for what I had done. Even though I felt the way that I did for him, I couldn't live with the fact that I had dishonored and disappointed God.

Once my secret rendezvous ended, I was alone again. My anger built up more and more towards my husband because I felt like he was to blame for what I had done. Even though he didn't make that decision for me, I felt if he had done right by me, my affair would not have happened. I never once took all of the blame. I had built a wall so tall that there was no way he could have reached over it or through it to get to me. If something bothered me, he would be the last to know. I opened up to strangers before opening up to him. I completely shut down on him.

All of the extra things that he liked for me to do in the bedroom, came to an end. Why would I make him happy when he broke my heart? I couldn't believe he was walking around like everything was okay. When I looked at him, it was with disgust in my eyes.

Jude thought everything was okay because I never expressed to him how I was feeling. I didn't realize how stuffing my emotions affected me in so many areas in my life. It stopped the communication and the intimacy was gone. I totally disconnected my body and my emotions from him.

For most of our marriage I fought a constant battle within myself. As I mentioned earlier, even though I said that I'd forgiven him, reflecting back on some of my actions, I realized that I really hadn't. I constantly prayed to God to help me with the hurt and pain that I had endured and to give me the attraction that I once had for him. But, it had to start with me. I had to not only trust God, but also forgive Jude. And I had to come against fear, which held me captive. Once I did those things, I knew that God would move. But until then, I was going to remain in captivity.

Now that God has shown me revelation through writing this book, I now know that truly forgiving someone is paramount. Forgiving will knock down barriers that the enemy uses to cause confusion in marriages, families and friendships.

I often wondered if I had died a year ago without forgiveness in my heart, would I have made it into Heaven? Would God let me in with the anger I felt towards people that had wronged me, lied on me, hurt and mistreated me? Wow! That's something to really think about.

Now that God has healed me from all of the hurt and pain that I carried for forty-one years, my mind is no longer foggy. I no longer feel lonely or think about the hurt that others caused me. Most of all, the intimacy and communication is great between my husband and me. I no longer accept anything that's going to make feel unworthy, because I am. We have to first love ourselves before we can love anyone else. People will treat us the way we allow them to. Not accepting that treatment is the key.

In the process of writing this book, my husband told me that he saw a difference in me. Hearing that made me feel good because it proved to me that God was working on me. And He did tell me that my book was going to be healing for me. Look at God. He is so amazing, good and awesome! We serve a mighty good God who loves us all. I now have joy in my heart and a peace of mind.

Your healing starts with you. Forgive those that have hurt or wronged you, and watch God move the mountains in your life. The word "forgive" means to wipe the slate clean, to pardon, to cancel a debt. When we wrong someone, we should seek his or her forgiveness in order for the relationship to be restored. It is important to remember that forgiveness is not granted because a person deserves to be forgiven. Instead, it is an act of love, mercy and grace. How we act toward that person may change. It doesn't mean we will put ourselves back into a harmful situation or that we suddenly accept or approve of the person's continued wrong behavior. It simply means we release them from the wrong they committed against us. We forgive them because God forgave us.

There's never a wrong time for a heart check. Is there someone in your life that you say you have forgiven, but really haven't? If so, pray this prayer with me.

Heavenly Father,

I pray You help me to identify any un-forgiveness that's in my heart. Help me to remember that forgiveness is not a one-time action, but a way of life. In Jesus' Name, Amen.

Scriptures
Matthew 18:21-22

"Then came Peter to him, and said, Lord, how oft shall my brother sin against me, and I forgive him? till seven times? Jesus saith unto him, I say not unto thee, Until seven times: but, Until seventy times seven." (KJV)

Chapter Nine – The Healing Process

When God told me to write this book based on my life, I found myself, like Moses, asking a lot of questions. I asked Him, *How will my life help to heal others?*

I know that when God calls us for something, it's for a reason and it will be successful. So, when He speaks, you need to move or you will miss your breakthrough and your blessing.

After God revealed to me that he wanted me to write a book based on my life, He woke me up one morning at 2:16 A.M. and placed an Emerald green book before me with the word "Naked" on it.

I asked God, "Why do you want me to name it, Naked?" He didn't answer me at the moment. I tried everything that I could think of to find the connection between the word naked and Emerald green, but I couldn't come up with anything. So, throughout the day I constantly asked God, "Why?" I anxiously waited on an answer from Him. I knew that He would reveal it to me, but I didn't know when.

Later that day around one o'clock, I decided to look up the word "Naked" to see if there was another meaning other than what I already knew. The definition read: nude or no covering. About an hour later, God revealed the reason and it was because He wanted to expose everything that I had gone through to heal his people.

As the day went by, I designed my book cover in my mind out of excitement. But, for some reason, God removed the vision that I had and placed that same Emerald green book before me. I asked God why He kept flashing that green book before me. Of course, He didn't answer me at that moment. God is a God of perfect timing.

I patiently waited on God's answer. I was so excited that I could hardly sleep. On my way to church the following Sunday I told God that I was expecting a word from Him. I had a feeling in my spirit that God was going to speak to me that day. Once praise and worship began during Sunday service, we sang a song about healing.

What you have to understand is that normally the colored lights on the stage, and the images on the monitor, coincide with each song that the congregation sings. God directed my eyes on the screen, which was the color green. He revealed to me that the color green represented healing, which the choir also happened to be singing about. He told me that my book would heal His people. I wept and praised God uncontrollably. I was amazed that God was communicating with me the way that He was. I thought to myself, *now everything makes sense.* He wanted to expose what I've been through to heal His people. God is so good to me!

We all were placed here for a reason. Are you serving your purpose in life? If not, what are you waiting for? God is waiting on you to ask Him to reveal your purpose in life. And, watch how He moves while answering. I'm a living witness.

Once we ask, we must humble ourselves, trust in God and wait on Him to move in our lives. When He speaks to you, please listen and be obedient.

When God decided to reveal to me my purpose, I didn't know what to expect next. As He continued communicating to me in a profound way, He showed me how messed up and damaged I was. After asking God how He expected me to write a book to heal His people when I was so messed up, He took me through my healing process.

While writing this book, He broke down everything that was holding me in bondage. His Spirit took my thoughts back to the people that I had trusted and loved the most, and how they'd hurt me. I couldn't understand how people could be so cold-hearted.

I remembered being told several times as a child, and as an adult, that I was too friendly. So, being told that on several occasions, I questioned myself. Maybe, I *am* too friendly! Maybe, that's why I'm always getting hurt! What I didn't realize is that I allowed those people to plant a negative seed in my spirit, tempting me to not develop close relationships.

Because of the hurt that others caused me, I isolated myself from everyone. But, God allowed that to happen because of the plans that He had for my life. God took me through a process of separation, which He used that time to make me over and minister to me. He taught me that it's okay to be nice, but be mindful of the people that I allow in my life. What I didn't know is that He was preparing me for my purpose. God will remove people from our lives that don't mean us any good. So, stop trying to fix what's not fixable. Forgive your brothers and sisters and move on.

God also showed me that there was nothing wrong with me being friendly. The enemy worked to devour and tear down my friendliness by using people to compromise the gift of "Love" that God had given me. The devil knew that God had plans for me so he attacked me from every angle of my life—my entire life. While writing this book, he used people and different situations to try to distract me so I couldn't focus on what God had assigned me to do. God revealed to me that I couldn't control how people felt or what they said about me, and that I must know that it's not them, but the enemy using them.

I had to stop worrying about the things I had no control over. I stood boldly before the enemy while standing on the Word of God that says, "No weapon formed against me shall prosper;"(Isaiah 54:17). I took back my joy, finances and my family. I thanked God for revelation. I will never compromise my friendly demeanor, which I believe is a gift of "Love" that God has given me, for anything or anybody again.

In the beginning of the writing/healing process, I thought about some of the things that were said and done to me. The anger I felt was coming back. Thinking on it literally took me back to that place. My husband's affair, my affair, anger, embarrassment, guilt and shame flooded me. Why? Because I hadn't forgiven him and I hadn't let it go. God constantly revealed to me how forgiving people and letting go of things was so important. He did this through sermons at church, through others and to me specifically while writing this book. My lack of forgiveness controlled my everyday life, which caused unhappiness. I didn't realize how I was allowing the enemy to control me.

The enemy likes to focus on your past and remind you of it often, which will keep you from moving ahead. Now that I'm living by the Word of God, Satan has to flee. Needless to say, I know that he's going to try to attack me in some other ways, but I will stand and let God fight my battles. I know that it's not my battle, it's God's. I was caught in the middle of a spiritual warfare between God and Satan. I was no longer allowing the enemy to have any control over my life. That's why it's important for us to live our lives according to His word. Don't allow the devil to come in and destroy what God has given you. Always allow the Word of God to dwell and prosper in your life.

Being judged throughout my life was challenging. I believed that people misunderstood me, didn't know my struggles and didn't know what I'd been through. So, when God told me to write a book based on my experiences that was my opportunity to expose myself for the person I really am.

I'd been through so much it seemed like I'd never had a break. I'm no different from anyone else and I wasn't ashamed of sharing with the world that I was once lost, had dishonored God, struggled with insecurities, committed adultery and allowed the enemy to control my life. I believed that was the reason God chose me for this assignment. I didn't know that expressing how I felt through writing was going to be therapeutic for me, but He knew.

Going through my healing process, I have learned several things that may help you as you allow God to heal you. Here is a list of steps to follow:

1. Be more compassionate to others and myself.
2. Be honest with yourself.
3. Never compromise God's gifts to you, including your personality.
4. Be humble and quick to admit when you are wrong.
5. Love your enemies and forgive quickly.

Are you ready to start the healing process or are you already on the journey to healing? If so, pray this prayer with me.

Heavenly Father,

I pray that You will walk with me through this healing process. Guide me through the steps that I need to take on this new journey in my life. Thank you, In Jesus' Name, Amen.

Scriptures
Jeremiah 17:14
"Heal me, O LORD, and I shall be healed; save me, and I shall be saved: for thou art my praise." (KJV)

1 Peter 2:24
"Who his own self bare our sins in his own body on the tree, that we, being dead to sins, should live unto righteousness: by whose stripes ye were healed." (KJV)

Chapter Ten – My Testimony

One night while I was working at the Marriott on the evening shift from 4 P.M.-12:30 A.M. my car wasn't working so I had to catch the bus. After a certain time the buses would run every hour, rather than every ten to fifteen minutes. Well, I missed the bus that I would normally catch that would let me off on a street that had plenty of lights and people hanging out. But because it was already late, and I didn't want to wait another hour for the bus, I decided to catch a different bus. When I got off of the bus, the street was basically pitch black and there was an uneasy feeling in my stomach so I asked God to protect me on my way home.

As I walked down this dark and secluded street, an SUV with a loud engine, and about four to five guys in it, pulled up and someone said, "Hey Shorty, do you need a ride?" Politely, I told them I didn't have far to go. With a smile on my face, I thanked them. To be honest, I don't think they were able to see my smile, that's how dark it was.

My heart was racing a mile a minute. I didn't want to be rude or mean, because I didn't want to make them angry. Once they pulled off and turned the corner, the Holy Spirit spoke loudly, saying, "RUN."

So I did, as fast as I could, in high heels and a flowing skirt. Once I made it to the first corner I came to, I turned left. In the middle of the block, there was an empty lot with grass taller than me. As soon as I made it to the middle of the block and was able to hide behind the grass, I could see them riding by slowly, trying to find me. I was hoping and praying that they didn't turn on the street that I was hiding. Once they realized that they couldn't locate me, they pulled off at full speed. When I saw that they were no longer in the area, I ran home as fast I could. Isn't God good!

At the age of 18, I was pregnant with my first child and was living at my aunt's home. She only had a two-bedroom home, which required me to sleep on the sofa. When it was time for bed, sometimes my cousin would ask me to come and lay in the bed with her so we could joke around and laugh.

One particular night, I climbed in the bed with her, her sister, and her baby. We joked and laughed for about forty-five minutes to an hour and then we fell asleep. While I was asleep, I felt someone's hand in my panties. When I opened my eyes, squinting, I could see a man standing over me, wearing a black jacket with the hood over his head. I was trying to figure out, who he was. I didn't want to panic because I wasn't sure if he had a weapon or not, so I played it calm. I immediately started squirming, to let him know that I was awake, but with my eyes barely opened. When he realized that I wasn't asleep, he backed up to the doorway and just stood there and watched me. Then, he walked away and left out of the backdoor of the house.

I immediately woke my cousin and explained to her what had just transpired, but she didn't believe me. She said, "If you're telling the truth, let's walk through the house to see if someone is in here." I said, "Okay, but I'm not going first, you are!"

As we walked through the house, we discovered that the backdoor was unlocked. She said, "That doesn't mean anything, maybe my mom left it unlocked." I tried everything in me to get her to believe me, but she wouldn't. Keep in mind that we were just joking and playing around. She said, "If you're not lying, go tell my mom."

Once I made it to my aunt's room, I knocked three times. On that third knock, my cousin started screaming at the top of her lungs, jumping up and down. She then ran down the hallway towards us. Then, I panicked and ran into my cousin's room and locked her in the hallway. I could hear her on the other side of the door crying uncontrollably and trying to explain to her mom what had just happened. She said, "There's the man standing in the backyard looking through the kitchen window."

I believe that he had every intention on coming back and was just giving me time to go back to sleep. Now, just think if God hadn't used my cousin to call me in the room. I would've been in the living room alone and could've been raped or possibly killed.

Even though I survived both events, they left me fearful. Not to mention, I slept fully clothed for years. God protected me every time so why shouldn't I trust Him with my life? I have every reason not to doubt Him. With all of the mishaps in my life, He'd always protected me from harm, even the harm that I didn't know about.

God chose and trusted me to bring forth His word through my book. He took me from the familiar to the unknown. He is using my life experiences to encourage you. And wants you to know that He's able to do exceeding abundantly above all that we ask or think, according to the power that works within us. (Ephesians 3:20)

God is. a healer and a peacemaker and you are more than a conqueror through Christ Jesus (Romans 8: 37). Today, I can honestly say that I'm brand new in Christ Jesus. The freedom and joy that I have in my heart are unexplainable. The love that I have for Him is untouchable.

Take a moment to think about all of the things that you have been through in your life, and then think about how God brought you through. Yes, it was tough, but it was necessary. You made it, right? God allows us to go through trials and tribulations because He wants us to solely depend on Him. He wants to draw us closer to Him and to make us stronger. He wants you to be able to share your testimony so it can encourage someone else.

The love that I have for God has grown and has brought my husband and me closer together. The things that used to bother me don't anymore. I constantly talk and think about how good God is. Watching how He's moving in my life confirms that His grace and mercy follows me my entire life, and He has given me favor.

When I think about the goodness of God, I get emotional. I know that He's with me every step of the way each and every day. I can't get enough of His pure and genuine love.

Take a moment and thank God for the times that you know He spared your life.

Heavenly Father,

Thank You for the times that You spared my life, even when I didn't deserve it. Thank You for loving me in spite of the mess that I was once in. In Jesus' Name, Amen!

Scripture
Revelation 12:11

"And they overcame him by the blood of the Lamb, and by the word of their testimony; and they loved not their lives unto the death." (KJV)

Chapter Eleven – Walking in My Purpose

I remember watching Bishop T.D. Jakes on "Oprah's Life Class" when he spoke about his new book "Instinct." Listening to him teach on following our instincts inspired me to want to hear more, so I purchased his book. In the book he spoke about not being afraid to step outside of the cage and knowing our purpose. This inspired me to ask God, *"What's my purpose?"*

Once I decided to believe for greater, God started moving. Most of the time we get comfortable in our everyday lifestyle and don't want it disrupted. We are afraid to take chances. As I mentioned earlier in the text, I have only completed my high school education, which I feel limits me from some of the things that I want to achieve. I once applied for a job that required a college degree and felt discouraged and not smart enough when I didn't get it. However, I made up in my mind that I wasn't going to carry mail or work for someone else for the rest of my life. So, I started speaking, "I am the head and not the tail." "I am the boss and not the employee."

When God instructed me to write this book, I knew that I had to be obedient even though I was afraid. I felt like writing a book was completely outside of my element as well as God using my life experiences to minister to His people. Going from carrying mail to becoming a first-time author is a big leap in careers.

Being obedient proved to God that I trusted him. Working a full time job and writing took a lot of sacrificing. I got hardly any sleep. While walking down the street delivering mail, I constantly thought about how good God was and how He was using me. I was honored that He chose me to do this. He had been waiting on me to come to Him. I knew that the instructions I followed determined the future I'd create. I didn't know that my blessings and my purpose would be birthed out of trials and tribulations.

Even though I didn't see what God had in store for me, I stood on faith. I spoke my future into existence. "Now faith is the substance of things hoped for, the evidence of things not seen." (Hebrews 11:1)

Here are a couple of things to remember when asking God to show you your purpose:

1. Believe for greater
2. Listen for instructions, have faith and follow them
3. Be prepared for distractions
4. Trust God to overcome the distractions

In the process of writing this book the enemy tried to distract me with family issues and conflict at work. Sometimes when my spirit was down, God would send someone to minister to me. It would usually be through a sermon or through prayer. We have to remember that the enemy would do anything to keep us from doing what God has set before us.

One day my husband went to the doctor because he was having severe headaches. The doctor told him that he had a pinched nerve in his shoulder. As months went by, he continued to have severe headaches, which caused him not to get much sleep at night. I informed my husband that he needed to go to the doctor again and request an MRI. Finally, he went back to the doctor and did as I asked. Once the results came back, he was diagnosed with Chiari Malformation.

Chiari Malformation is a condition in which brain tissue extends into your spinal canal. It occurs when part of your skull is abnormally small or misshapen, pressing on your brain and forcing it downward. The doctor told him that the only way he could help this issue is through having surgery.

Once the surgery was scheduled, I knew in my heart that everything would be okay. I declared healing in the Name of Jesus! Of course, a week before the surgery, the enemy started putting negative thoughts in my head. One morning I tossed and turned, thinking the worst. Later that morning I said to myself, *I got to get it together. My husband will live and not die!*

But, throughout the day, I kept having negatives thoughts. I was emotional and this made my heart sad. I kept going back and forth with myself; therefore, lacking faith. That's how the enemy operates. He wanted to distract me so that I would doubt God.

God got me together real fast. Later that evening I received a call from a high school friend. She called to pray a prayer of agreement with me for my husband. God used her to tell me that if I was going to pray to God for healing for my husband, there was no need to worry; but, if I was going to worry, there was no need to pray. God is so good! He knew exactly how I was feeling, so he used her to tell me to leave it in His hands and to stand on faith. After praying, I felt so much better. I thanked God for His love, mercy and grace.

My husband facing surgery made me realize how much I really loved him and it showed me how much he loved and appreciated me. I don't think he realized how much he appreciated me until then. When the doctor came to the waiting room after the surgery to talk to my mother-in-law and I, my heart was pounding but I was anxious to know my husband's status. Once he told me that everything went well, I thanked God immediately. God is good, amazing and awesome!

God allows certain things to happen in our lives for a reason. I believe that He allowed this surgery to take place because He knew that it would draw us closer to Him, draw us closer to each other, and to show others that He's a healer.

If you are ready to walk in purpose, here are a few things to remember:

1. You must be dedicated and committed to personal change
2. Don't be afraid to walk through open doors and take new opportunities
3. Remember that you represent Christ at all times, so walk in love

I am so glad that you have walked with me as I became naked before God and started my journey to purpose. If somewhere along the way of reading this book you decided to unstuff, forgive, break patterns and heal with me, then you are on the right path. Let's pray for the strength to continue on this journey.

Heavenly Father,

I pray that You direct me in the path that You have for me. I want to strip naked before You, so that I can be healed and see clearly where You want me to go. Give me the strength that I will need along this journey. In Jesus' Name, Amen.

Scriptures
Matthew 7:7-8

"Ask, and it shall be given you; seek, and ye shall find; knock, and it shall be opened unto you: For every one that asketh receiveth; and he that seeketh findeth; and to him that knocketh it shall be opened." (KJV)

Matthew 6:33

"But seek ye first the kingdom of God, and his righteousness; and all these things shall be added unto you." (KJV)

A Note from the Author

Thank you so much for reading my story. I pray that it was a blessing to you. I would love to connect with you and hear more about your story. Like my Facebook page, Romella Vaughn. God bless you today and always!

Made in the USA
San Bernardino, CA
03 April 2015